DATE DUE

DEMCO 38-297

The U.S. F-117A stealth fighter attacked targets in Iraq. General H. Norman Schwarzkopf III explains the battle plan for Operation Desert Storm.

An A-7 fighter flies over an aircraft carrier in the Persian Gulf. A marine M-68 tank (inset left) leads a group of vehicles armed with antitank missile launchers. Artillery, such as the Dragon (inset right), was very effective in combat.

Cornerstones of Freedom

The Story of
THE PERSIAN GULF WAR

By Leila Merrell Foster

CP CHILDRENS PRESS®
CHICAGO

Hundreds of people sought refuge in the U.S. Embassy compound
in Kuwait City when Iraq invaded on August 2, 1990.

Library of Congress Cataloging-in-Publication Data

Foster, Leila Merrell.

   The story of the Persian Gulf War / by Leila Merrell
Foster.
      p.   cm. — (Cornerstones of freedom)
   Summary: Examines the causes and events of the
Persian Gulf War that followed Iraq's invasion of Kuwait in
1990.
   ISBN 0-516-04762-0
   1.   Persian Gulf War, 1991—Juvenile literature.
[1.   Persian Gulf War, 1991.   2.   Iraq-Kuwait Crisis,
1990-]   I.   Title.   II.   Series.
DS79.72.F47   1991
956.704'3—dc20   91-4037
                                               CIP
                                                AC

PHOTO CREDITS

AP/Wide World Photos—Cover, 1 (2 photos), 2 (left inset),
3, 4, 5 (top left and bottom right), 6, 7 (right), 8 (right), 9,
15, 18 (2 photos), 19 (left), 20 (left), 21 (2 photos), 22 (left),
23, 24 (right), 25, 27 (2 photos), 28 (top), 30 (2 photos)

Photri—2 (top and right inset), 11 (2 photos), 12 (2 photos),
13, 19 (right), 20 (right), 22 (right), 24 (top left and bottom
left), 25 (inset), 32

Reuters/Bettmann—7 (left), 16, 17, 26, 28 (bottom), 29
(2 photos)

UPI/Bettmann—8 (left)

Cover—Two American soldiers on dawn patrol somewhere
in Saudi Arabia

Page 3: The tank and the camel represent new and old
            methods of transportation in the desert.

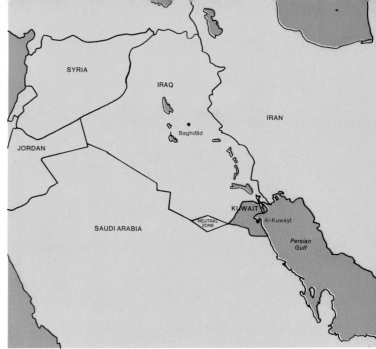

The television image (left) shows an Iraqi truck carrying soldiers and an armored personnel carrier in Kuwait. Map of Persian Gulf region (right)

On August 2, 1990, the citizens of Kuwait woke up to sounds of war. Tanks were rumbling down their streets, helicopters were flying overhead, and Iraqi soldiers were stopping cars and killing the occupants. The Kuwaitis were stunned by the attack. Why would their Muslim neighbor invade them?

Kuwait is a small country on the Arabian Peninsula at the head of the Persian Gulf. It shares borders with Iraq and Saudi Arabia. Iraq is twenty-four times the size of Kuwait and almost nine times as populous. The Iraqi army, led by Saddam Hussein, was the largest in the Middle East—about a million strong. Kuwait only had about 20,000 troops.

The Kuwaitis had supported Iraq during its eight-

Saddam Hussein

5

year war with Iran. Kuwait had poured money into that war. Nevertheless, Iraqi troops invaded Kuwait at dawn. After taking over the rich oil wells and the border ports, the Iraqi army moved quickly across the entire country and on toward Saudi Arabia.

Iraqi soldiers searched for members of Kuwait's ruling Al-Sabah family, but the emir (ruler) and the crown prince escaped to Saudi Arabia to set up resistance operations there. The emir's brother, Sheik Fahd Ahmed Al-Jabir Al-Sabah, was killed on the first day of the invasion while he was trying to defend the Dasman Palace.

Kuwaiti soldiers tried to defend their country, but the odds against them were overwhelming. Officers at the Ministry of Defense headquarters surrendered in an effort to save their three hundred men.

TV image shows a woman injured during the attack on Kuwait City.

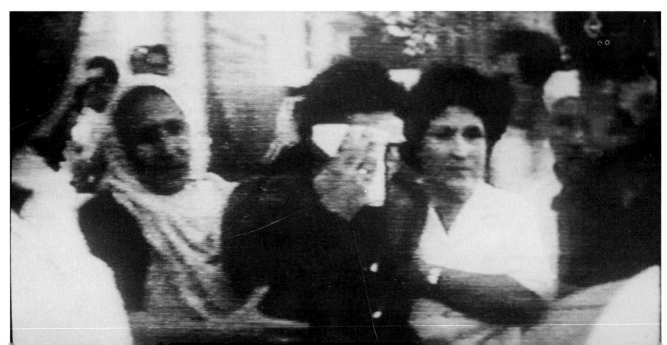

Kuwaitis killed during the invasion were buried in mass graves (left). Saddam Hussein (right) congratulates his troops in Kuwait.

But after taking their weapons, the Iraqis fired upon the unarmed Kuwaitis and in fifteen minutes all of them were dead or dying.

The Iraqi savagery was not limited to the military. Young men trying to flee the country with their families were seized. Women were attacked. Hospitals were invaded. Patients were disconnected from life-support systems, and hospital equipment was shipped to Iraq. Many people were left to die. Doctors were forced at gunpoint to work on Iraqis before they could care for Kuwaitis.

Over time, some Kuwaiti resistance was organized. In one tragic incident, as women and children marched in peaceful opposition to their conquerors, Iraqi soldiers fired into the crowd. A doctor reported that five children between the ages of four and ten were brought to his hospital for treatment, but only two of the youngsters could be saved.

Kuwaiti resistance groups helped their people and hid many foreigners who had been trapped in Kuwait.

Why did Iraq attack? Iraq had recently ended an eight-year war with Iran. That war is generally believed to have started with an Iraqi attack in September 1980, although Iraq claims that Iran began the conflict by shelling its border posts. Finally, in 1988, the two countries agreed to a cease-fire. After the years of fighting, there was little to show in the way of gains for either side.

Iraqi troops (right) at an anti-aircraft position. Thousands were killed or wounded during the Iran-Iraq war.

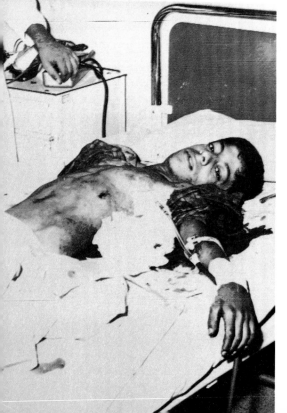

Saddam was cheered when the Iran-Iraq war ended.

Since 1979, Saddam Hussein had been the president of Iraq and the head of the Revolutionary Command Council, a governing junta that has controlled Iraq since the mid-1960s. But without the Iran-Iraq war to justify a strong political leader, Saddam Hussein faced requests from the Iraqi people for greater political freedom.

At first, Saddam seemed willing to increase opportunities for participation in the government. However, after the cease-fire in 1988, Iraqi troops moved against the Kurds, a minority people living in the north of Iraq who wanted their own separate territory. Some of the Kurds had sided with Iran against Iraq in hopes of gaining a homeland. Now

9

Iraq used troops and chemical weapons against the Kurds, killing 5,000 people and forcing hundreds of thousands to flee to Turkey and Iran.

Did Saddam Hussein invade Kuwait because he needed a war in order to control Iraq's government? At first, Iraq claimed that it was liberating Kuwaitis who wished to be freed from their autocratic emir. Later, when Iraq announced that it was annexing Kuwait, Hussein claimed that he was just taking back territory that historically had belonged to Iraq.

The Ottoman Empire had ruled much of the area, including Iraq, for centuries. Kuwait, once an Ottoman province, had been ruled by the Al-Sabah family since the late eighteenth century, and had been under British protection since 1897. When the Ottoman Empire broke up after World War I, Iraq also came under British protection.

Iraq became a kingdom in 1921 under the Hashemite family. When the Hashemite king was assassinated in 1958, a republic was proclaimed.

In 1961, when the British left, Kuwait became independent. At that time, Kuwait was admitted as a member of the Arab League (a coalition of Arab countries). In 1963, Kuwait became a member of the United Nations (UN).

However, Kuwait's independence seems to have

The museum (above) displayed many of Kuwait's treasures. Because of its oil wealth, Kuwait was able to irrigate and grow crops in the desert.

mattered little to the Iraqis. Kuwait had three things that were important to the Iraqis: oil, wealth, and ports. Saddam Hussein had complained that Kuwait was producing too much oil and thereby driving down the price at which Iraq could sell its own oil. To pacify Hussein, the Organization of Petroleum Exporting Countries (OPEC) reached an agreement on July 27, 1990, that raised the target price of oil.

In spite of OPEC's action, Saddam Hussein took Kuwait's oil field a few days later. Combined with Iraq's resources, Kuwait's oil would give Hussein control of 20 percent of the world's oil supply. Since the industrial nations needed oil to maintain their economic base, Hussein would gain tremendous power through control of this resource.

Wealth was another factor. The Gulf nations are aware that oil deposits—even the vast supplies with which they have been blessed—will eventually be used up. So, every year, Kuwait added 10 percent of its total revenue to its Reserve Fund for Future Generations (RFFG). This fund was not to be touched until the year 2001. By 1990, Kuwait had $100 billion invested abroad, and the return from these investments now exceeded the country's annual income from oil exports. These funds would have been a prize, indeed, had Saddam Hussein been able to get his hands on them. But when his forces invaded Kuwait, foreign countries froze these over-

Pipelines (left) carried Kuwait's oil to tankers moored in the Gulf. The oil fields at Mina Al Ahmadi (right) made the country rich.

Huge intake pipes carried seawater into Kuwait's desalination plants.

seas investments for use by the exiled Kuwaiti government, so Iraq was able to seize only the money in local banks. Private savings and assets in Kuwait were soon swept away by the Iraqis.

Iraq's need for Gulf ports was another reason for the invasion. Iraq's main water route to the Gulf, the Shatt-al-Arab, was clogged with the wreckage of ships after its war with Iran. The waterway would have to be dredged to be of use again. Iraq was building new ports but wanted the Kuwaiti islands of Bubiyan and Warbah to assure the safety of traffic into its ports. While Kuwait may have been willing to forgive some of the debt Iraq owed in order to keep Iraq happy, the emir could see no reason to give up Kuwaiti territory.

Psychological reasons may also explain Saddam Hussein's actions. It seems likely that he wanted to be viewed as a great Arab leader. His frequent tirades against the West and Israel were designed to influence the Arab masses. Many Arabs have hated the West from the times of the European invasions during the Crusades (between the 11th and 13th centuries). They were also dissatisfied with the Middle Eastern territorial settlements made by the Western powers after World War I. And many Arabs hate Israel for its occupation of disputed territory, for its treatment of the Palestinians, and for its victories over Arab armies.

Another reason for Hussein's actions may have been his expectation that he could get away with it. In the Middle East before World War I, it was not unusual for local tribes to raid each other's territory for camels and horses, which were the measure of wealth in those days. And in 1990, who would challenge Saddam Hussein? He had the largest army in the area. The industrial nations did not have adequate forces in the Middle East to stop him. In the climate of relief at the end of the Cold War between the West and the Soviet bloc, would any nation have the will to challenge him? The United States remembered Vietnam, and the Soviet Union remembered Afghanistan.

Saddam Hussein may have invaded Kuwait for all these reasons. What power he would have had if the world had let him take Kuwait and Saudi Arabia, against whose borders he had moved his troops. With both these oil-rich nations under his control, he would truly have been the Oil King, and the rest of the world would have had to do his will if they wanted his oil.

Iraq's neighbors in the Middle East were not blind to Saddam Hussein's ambitions. Many were not sorry that he was occupied for eight years in fighting against Iran. Israel, fearful of nuclear weapons in the hands of Saddam Hussein, bombed a reactor site in Iraq in 1981.

On the other hand, after the war between Iraq

President Hussein with his troops

Egypt's President Mubarak (left) met Saddam Hussein on July 24, 1990.

and Iran ended in 1988, it looked as though Hussein might want peace. Certainly, he wanted to buy foreign goods for the development of his country. And certainly the industrial nations were interested in selling Iraq such goods.

In 1990, when Saddam Hussein accused Kuwait and the neighboring United Arab Emirates of an "imperialist Zionist plan" in keeping oil prices low, Arab countries recognized the threat and tried to find a peaceful solution. Hussein said on July 17, "Iraqis will not forget the maxim that cutting necks is better than cutting the means of living. O God Almighty, be witness that we have warned them." Ten days later, the OPEC agreement more favorable to Iraqi interests was reached. On July 24, President Mubarak of Egypt tried to mediate the conflict.

Saddam Hussein told Mubarak then and U.S. ambassador April Glaspie later that he had "no intention of invading Kuwait."

On August 1, attempts to get Iraq and Kuwait to negotiate their differences were broken off by Iraq after only two hours. The next day, when Kuwait was invaded, the United States and other industrial nations condemned the attack, called for economic sanctions, and froze Kuwaiti and Iraqi assets in their countries.

By August 3, one day after the attack, both the

Iraqi tank carrying a picture of the emir of Kuwait rolls down the streets of Kuwait City. Kuwait's small army was no match for Iraq's military might.

U.S. Ambassador Thomas R. Pickering watches as Yemen's Ambassador Abdalla Saleh al Ashtal (above, at left) abstains from this vote. The United Nations Security Council (right) voted for economic sanctions against Iraq.

UN and the Arab League had approved resolutions condemning the Iraqi aggression against Kuwait. The UN Security Council vote was 14 to 0. The UN resolution condemned Iraq's invasion and called for immediate withdrawal. Yemen, an Arab country on the Arabian Peninsula, abstained from the UN vote. In the Arab League, 14 of the 21 members approved the resolution of condemnation.

By August 6, the UN voted economic sanctions by 13 to 0, with Cuba and Yemen abstaining. Iraq responded by moving troops south of Kuwait City, nearer the Saudi Arabian border. The Saudis then invited the United States to send troops to Saudi Arabia. President George Bush responded by

U.S. troops (left) prepare for war in Saudi Arabia. President George Bush (right) congratulates General Colin Powell, chairman of the Joint Chiefs of Staff.

launching Operation Desert Shield.

President Bush announced that he had taken this action "after perhaps unparalleled international consultation, and exhausting every alternative." He presented a four-point policy: (1) "immediate, unconditional, and complete withdrawal of all Iraqi forces from Kuwait"; (2) restoration of Kuwait's legitimate government; (3) commitment to the security and stability of the Persian Gulf; and (4) protection of the lives of American citizens abroad.

Saddam Hussein responded by announcing the annexation of Kuwait on August 8. On August 9, the UN Security Council declared the annexation null and void under international law.

Egyptian troops (left) in gas masks and French soldiers (right) represent two of the twenty-eight nations that sent troops to fight in the Persian Gulf War.

The UN nations took action. Britain, France, and the Arab countries of Egypt and Morocco sent military forces to Saudi Arabia. Several nations sent naval forces to the Gulf to support the sea embargo against Iraq. The European Community, Japan, Germany, and others offered financial support. By January 15—the UN deadline for Saddam Hussein to leave Kuwait—twenty-eight Allied countries had lined up against Iraq with an astounding array of military equipment.

With the Soviet Union and the United States no longer engaged in a power struggle, the UN Security Council was able to pass some twelve resolutions dealing with the Gulf crisis. Iraq was criticized for attempting to use foreign hostages as human shields in the event of war and for its treatment of foreign diplomats. During the period from before the invasion of Kuwait to the January 15 deadline, UN Secretary General Javier Pérez de Cuéllar, U.S. Secretary of State James Baker, and other world leaders made many attempts—without success—to negotiate a peace.

In the United States, oil prices rose, increasing its economic recession. The stock market, reflecting the concern about the Middle East unrest, went down. The U.S. Congress voted 416 to 0 to institute a trade embargo in August 1990. However, there were

President Hussein appeared with his European hostages on television.
Right: UN Secretary General Pérez de Cuéllar met with Iraqi foreign minister Taraq Aziz, at right.

differences of opinion about whether President Bush as commander in chief could order U.S. forces into action—as many presidents had—without Congress declaring war or authorizing the use of force. Ultimately, President Bush asked Congress to authorize him to send in the troops. The vote for this resolution was much closer (House: 250 to 183; Senate: 52 to 47) because some representatives believed the economic sanctions would succeed without the use of force.

Some people felt that any war was wrong. Others objected to this war because Kuwait was not a democracy, or because they believed we were fighting just for oil, or because a large percentage of people from minority groups were serving in the armed

The 155-mm self-propelled Howitzer (left) and the M-109 Howitzer (right) were two of the weapons used against Iraq.

forces or reserves. But by mid-January, two major polls showed that over 60 percent of the American people approved of the president's handling of the crisis as well as the use of military force by the United States.

When the January 15 deadline passed at midnight in Washington D.C., it was the morning of January 16 in the Middle East. That night—clear and dark with a new moon—was perfect for bombing. The airfields vibrated with the noise of the Allied airplanes taking off. In the early hours of January 17, bombs and missiles started hitting Baghdad, the capital of Iraq. Operation Desert Shield became

Anti-aircraft fire lights up Baghdad's night sky.

Operation Desert Storm. United States General H. Norman Schwarzkopf III told his troops, "My confidence in you is total; our cause is just. Now you must be the thunder and lightning of Desert Storm."

Civilians throughout the world were amazed at the television coverage of the raids on Baghdad. On their TV screens, they were seeing "live" pictures of the deadly fireworks of modern war. The massive force of twenty-eight nations was allied against Saddam Hussein. Their advanced weaponry gave new meaning to firepower.

Allied "smart bombs" hit strategic targets throughout Iraq, cut communications, and disabled

U.S. Patriot missiles (below left) and Iraqi Scud missiles (bottom left).
This Scud missile (below, right) killed three and wounded seventy people when it landed in Tel Aviv, Israel.

The color banner atop each tank helps the airborne Marine Cobra gunship identify friendly tanks. An F-14 (inset) launches a Phoenix missile.

the front line artillery. Air superiority sent many Iraqi planes fleeing to the safety of Iran, while others remained grounded in the protection of civilian areas.

In retaliation, the Iraqis launched Scud missiles into Israel and Saudi Arabia. There were fears that Israel would strike back, which would put the Arab members of the Allied forces—Israel's traditional enemies—in an awkward position. But Israel did not attack, and fortunately Patriot missiles knocked out most of the Iraqi Scuds.

Then, at 4 A.M. on February 24, Gulf time, the land war began. Allied forces launched an attack into Kuwait. Other troops moved far to the west,

As this huge sand map shows, the Iraqi leaders expected an attack from the Gulf. Most of their artillery and chemical weapons were positioned along the coastline.

around the heavily fortified front lines and into Iraq. Troops were sent north to the Tigris-Euphrates Valley, about a hundred miles from Baghdad, to block Iraqi supplies from coming in and to prevent Iraqi troops from retreating along that route. Meanwhile, some of Iraq's best troops were kept on the Gulf coast because of fears of an Allied attack from the water. Because their air force was grounded, the Iraqis had no way of knowing what the Allied forces were doing. Some one hundred hours after the land attack began, a temporary cease-fire was declared.

On February 27, 1991, just six weeks after the air war had started, Kuwait was liberated.

President Bush, in his address to the American people after the war began, spoke of the future: "We have before us the opportunity to forge for ourselves and for future generations a new world order, a world where the rule of law, not the law of the jungle, governs the conduct of nations."

Saddam Hussein had promised a "scorched earth" policy—total destruction—in Kuwait if he was attacked. He kept his promise. Oil was poured into the Gulf and oil wells were set on fire by Iraqi troops. He created an ecological disaster. The losses from the burning oil wells continue to increase the cost to the Kuwaitis.

Iraq deliberately blew up oil wells and pipelines. The environmental damage they did to the air and water in the Gulf will take years to undo.

Iraqi prisoners (above) guarded by Saudi troops.
Two Kuwaitis examine a ruined desalination plant
that supplied much-needed water to Kuwait City.

The Iraquis destroyed the power plant (left) that supplied electricity to Kuwait City. Sheik Jabir al Sabah, the emir of Kuwait, raises his hands as he returns home.

Iraquis also stole some $20 billion in goods from Kuwait and caused at least $25 billion worth of damage to buildings and equipment. Although the country's immense wealth will be used in rebuilding, Kuwait faces many problems. Tensions exist between Kuwaitis who remained in their country and fought in the resistance and Kuwaitis who rode out the war in comparative luxury in foreign countries. The Kuwaiti government has been criticized for its inability to meet the needs of residents, and also for its slowness in giving more rights to the people. How will the government deal with those who are asking for a more democratic society? How will the

Kuwaitis protect themselves in the future? What will happen to the many foreign workers who lived in Kuwait before the war?

Iraq also suffered great damage from the air attacks. On April 6, Iraq accepted the UN cease-fire resolution. The continuing UN economic sanctions are a signal to the Iraqi army that Iraq will not be rebuilt while Saddam Hussein stays in power. However, instead of ousting Hussein, the army turned its weapons against the Shiites—Iraqis living in the south who belong to a minority Muslim faction—and against the Kurds in the north. Vicious fighting in the south sent over 27,000 refugees streaming toward Saudi Arabia. Over 1 million Iraqi

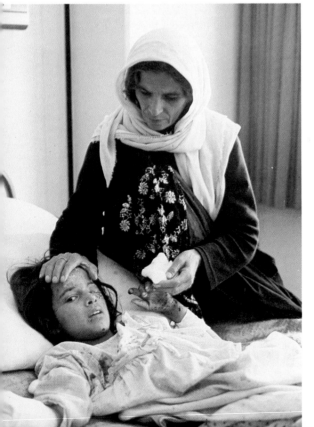

This young girl (left) lost her right hand and left eye when Iraqi troops attacked Kurdish rebels in Dohuk, Iraq. Millions of Kurds (below) fled Iraq seeking safety in Turkey and Iran.

Kurds, mindful of Iraq's previous use of chemical warfare against them, fled over the mountains to the Turkish and Iranian borders. Providing supplies for these refugees and protecting them from the Iraqi army posed a difficult problem.

Among the Arab allies, will the Western nations be viewed as saviors or meddlers? What will happen to the economic stability of countries that must now pay for the war and economic sanctions? How will defense needs and defense personnel be viewed in the future?

Will the Arab countries be under greater pressure to change their ways of ruling and living? Who will take over the power in this region if Iraq is no longer the major military force? Will Israel face a stronger and more unified Arab front, or will the Arabs be less supportive of the Palestinians, who allied themselves with Iraq? What will happen to Arab countries that did not support the Allied war effort—like Yemen and Jordan?

If militarily weak nations are to feel safe in the presence of strong ones, the international community must be willing to condemn aggression and find satisfactory ways of enforcing a just peace. The hope for the future is that the UN will be better able to keep the peace now that the world has seen the force that can be unleashed against an aggressor.

Cheering troops
from the combined
UN forces celebrate
the liberation
of Kuwait.

INDEX

About the Author

Leila Merrell Foster is a lawyer, United Methodist minister, and clinical psychologist with degrees from Northwestern University and Garrett Evangelical Theological Seminary. She is the author of books and articles on a variety of subjects.